GIN AND GARDENIAS

A MEMOIR OF DESIRE, LOVE, AND LOSS

POEMS BY

A. SCOTT HENDERSON

FpS
GREENVILLE, S.C.
2015

Copyright © 2015 by A. Scott Henderson

All rights reserved. No part of this book may be used or reproduced in any manner without written permission except for brief quotations in articles or reviews. Proper credit required.

Requests for permission should be addressed to:

Fiction Addiction Publishing Services
1175 Woods Crossing Rd., #5
Greenville, S.C. 29607
864-675-0540
www.fiction-addiction.com
www.fpspublishing.com

ISBN: 978-1-934216-77-4 (print edition)
ISBN: 978-1-934216-95-8 (electronic edition)

Library of Congress Control Number: 2015948103

Printed in the United States of America

Section images and the photos from which they were derived courtesy of the author

Book and cover design by Vally Sharpe of FPS

Author photo courtesy of Carol Sutton

For J.A., R.H., and R.P.

CONTENTS

CLEAVED	XI

I - DESIRE ARRIVING — 1

THE KISSING VIRUS, 1968	3
HOW TO TREAT A BOY	4
COSTUMED	5
MIDDLE ONE	6
I'M ALWAYS SILENT	7
DIFFERENT DRUMMING	8
WITH MY BROTHER IN DISNEY WORLD	9
MAGIC PILL TALK	10
BOYS IN GREEK-LETTERED SHIRTS	11
ARTICHOKES	12
ALTAR CALL	13
GIN AND GARDENIAS	14
SISSY MYTHS	15
NEEDLE IN, NEEDLE OUT	16
QUESTION TIME	17
WATER WASHES HANDS	18
OUT OF LOVE	19
I CAN USUALLY TELL	20
BEYOND CITY LIMITS	21

II - STEALING LONELINESS FROM THE NIGHT — 23

RED SHOELACES IN THE BIBLE BELT, 1986	25
ALL ALONG	26
FLAUNTING IT	27
SACRED OBJECTS SHOULDN'T LEAVE	28
SIBYL	29

THIS FROZEN PLACE	30
DEDICATIONS	31
CLOSETS	32
WITH OR WITHOUT PROPS	33
STICKING	34
MAKING WINE	35
JOINED	36
HOWLING ALONE	37
HAVING DRINKS AT THE POINSETT HOTEL	38
HELICOPTER OVER HAWAII	39
MAHJONG ("SPARROW GAME")	40

III - IN DEEPEST SLEEP — 41

THREE MINUTES, 2010	43
KINDLING	44
A POLITICAL ACT	45
POSTMORTEMS	46
THIS MORE OF ME	47
WITHOUT PERMISSION	48
CLOCKS	49
LEFT IN THE PACK	50
I'LL WAIT	51
ALONG A BACKYARD PATH	52
ADRIFT	53
DREAMS, YOU SAID	54
BACKSEAT ASHES	55
BOXES	56
SANDS OF KITTY HAWK	57
THINKING BAREFOOT THOUGHTS	58
THE CASTLE	59

IV - Reviving Rhythms   61

    Click to Enter   63
    Dancing in L.A.   64
    Self Fashioning   65
    Basic Math   66
    Dated   67
    The Flower of Southern Manhood   68
    I Can Leave Anything   69
    Hunting (Muscle Beach, CA)   70
    One Nightstand   71
    Pounding on Top   72
    A Woman with Becoming Features   73
    Choosing Fruit   74
    By Mixing Pink and Blue   75
    Unnatural   76
    Once Before   77
    Down South, 2015   78

Acknowledgments   81
About the Poet   83

Cleaved

I'm cleaved from myself

the child in a photograph
baby teeth gone
a gap waiting for self-awareness

which overwhelms when
it comes

negotiating the distance
between man and boy

the same smile
he and I
one to the other cleaved

a word
a life
conceiving their
opposites.

I
Desire Arriving

The greatest thing in the world is to know how to belong to oneself.

— Montaigne, *Essays*

The Kissing Virus, 1968

1.

The teacher sends my
homework home,
writing notes in her
knowing hand,
saying I'm special—
a boy who plays with girls

though I couldn't have gotten sick
from them:

it's the virus that loves to kiss.

During the gauzy haze of these
first-grade days,
I've had chills, aches, cherry Jello

dreaming of the three-day trip we took to
Silver Springs and Weeki Wachee—

albino alligators
a glass-bottom boat
water skiers stacked in pyramids
Kodak Instamatics aimed at
reptiles and magnolias
cotton candy turning my brother's face
into a pink disgrace—

but all I did was
stare
at men who bared
their brawny chests.

2.

My illness lingers on

even when
the Jello's gone.

How to Treat a Boy

As if I've missed
just to make him mad,
he shoves me on
my knees
to taste his playground
dirt:

You swing like a girl

screams this Goliath with
fists and cleated kicks,
branding me a traitor
to my t-ball teammates,
who'll thank him when he's
less irate
for showing them
without debate

how to treat a boy

who swings like
me.

Costumed

Prowling alone
down perilous streets,
stuffing candy
in pillow-cased fear,
ignoring my mother's
decree:

*You're too old for
that.*

A bleached-white sheet
swirls around me,
refusing to disguise
my lilting lack of swagger—

I'm Casper the Friendly Ghost
(The friendliest ghost you know),
suddenly attacked by sixth-grade
cannibals:

Faggot!

My face disfigured with
familiar tears
another test of manhood
failed—

a grieving self-deceiving
boy

telling himself:

*You're too old for
that.*

Middle One

Three umbrella-crowded boys

waiting with fuzzied upper-lips and
barely hairy legs

two of them claiming
they've *gone all the way*

masculinity held tight
like teeth in braces.

I've picked a large umbrella
to put me in the

middle

feeling my companions'
heat

fantasizing a gentle touch or
loving kiss

watching their pushing shoving
racing roughness.

Left alone
the umbrella hopes

for rain again tomorrow.

I'm Always Silent

A tawny, scrawny tribe
soaked in gym class sweat

giggling at *titular* and *titillate*

squeaky voices obsessed with
bra-covered flesh,
infantilized and paralyzed
by mid-pubescence.

I'm always silent when they
say
how much they want them
in their hands and mouths

averting my eyes
from shower-room bodies,
fearing they'll detect
my interest,
cowering against mildewed tiles
of junior high shame,
towel-snapped pain
aflame on my skin—

picked apart
and scarred within

by boys who drool
over burgeoning breasts.

Different Drumming

Uniforms pinned and hemmed
rehearsals ego-smudged
trombones slick with oil
mouthpieces tasting of spit
collars dampened black
shoes struggling in halftime mud

a sweaty bus befogged by
adolescents

where I kiss
my shirtless sophomore crush

then the rise

fingertips touching
his proudly stubbled face—

desire arriving like
a poem
unannounced

an impatient
improvisation.

With My Brother in Disney World

We're twin penguins
squinting behind glasses,
high school seniors swaddled in
sweaty tuxedoes,
a raucous rite with lukewarm beer
and overpriced pot,
our photo taken at dawn by an
underpaid mouse.

You look like Dad teaching us
how to shave,
our faces burning when he changed the topic from
trimming beards to having sex,
Old Spice and Salem cigarettes scenting his
suntanned hands.

That was the year you started playing
Little League

and I didn't miss a single game,
bored by fidgeting fathers with their
hopes for base-running sons,
preferring the wine-woozy mothers
who talked about men they'd undressed
at the gym.

Say cheese!

A flashbulb blinds our eyes,
and all I can see

is the part of me
that lives in you—

dreaming of the cards you'll get
To Dad

and aching
as the orange-squeezed sun slowly rises
on that long bus ride home.

Magic Pill Talk

1.

Metal chairs and padded walls
listen to us talk in tell-all tones,
daring the campus counselor
(a sorcerer's apprentice)
to spring her well-sprung trap:

*Would you take a magic pill
to make you straight?*

Blond hair blue eyes
in shorts and sweatshirt answers
Hell yes I'd take two
but swears he doesn't need them,
making a music major yell
Bull shit,
our digressions filling
the hour
with cuckoo-clock
confessions.

2.

We're laughing afterward at a
syrup-stained table,
the thin-grinned hostess hissing
Them fairies again,
when a freshman swimmer from Sarasota
sits beside me,
pressing his knee against my
willing leg—

and I'm thinking,
What a stupid question.

Boys in Greek-Lettered Shirts

play countless games on
outdoor courts,
packs of dogs who think they're
wolves,
hurling *homo* as they
grab, shove, score

entangling arms and legs
to make the winning dunk.

I crash their parties on full-moon nights,
Tallahassee bacchanals where
black-faced minstrels and strains of Dixie
compete as Old-South interludes—
over-muscled and under-bred,
our hosts delight in Gulf Coast oysters,
slimy raw and chased by beer,
allaying thoughts of being queer or
someone's Guinevere.

Shitfaced drunk is what it takes
to make them act the part
of gallant cavaliers,
kissing all the sweet camellias
before they grope them
with their paws.

But these benighted knights are
always sober
when they play their games
with other *boys*:

they grab, shove, score

entangling arms and legs
in crowded canine beds.

Artichokes

1.

The first three courses are
served without a fuss:
crayfish soup (*bisque* we self-correct)
salad minus lettuce
pimento cheese on toasted bread

but the fourth one is a
mystery
green and gray and oddly curled

mother and son
sitting in dread
afraid to make
a fatal mistake.

2.

We'd braved delays for
several days—

transmission trouble in Orlando,
flooded roads around Mobile,
greasy mechanics who leered at her
and laughed at me—

finally arriving where the crescent river
empties muddy secrets.

Yet she can't accept
what I won't confess—

a shameful cross she'd bear for life.

So we eat the unfamiliar dish,
including tough and bitter leaves

unrelenting thistles
that choke our silent conversation.

Altar Call

Ranting shepherd
smiling sheep

Sodomy Sodomize Sodomites

wooden pews
pointed stakes
dogma spewed in August heat

Burn them!

from Leviticus
from Romans
from a sermon praised in seminary

It's in the Bible

Confederate flags
the Body of Christ
grape juice spilled on Sunday ties
hoarse and needing more

They want your little boys

hands raised
tears shed
a final hymn
no spit left

Thou bidst me to come
just as I am

starched collar
bloody knees
I leave before they finish—

unforgiven and
unforgiving.

Gin and Gardenias

Dogwoods surround the house where
four of us eat dessert
rum raisin pie in the tea-sweetened South,
a brown-sugar buzz joining the gin that's
pounding my head.

I wear khaki pants and a short sleeve shirt
allowing a glimpse of my blond haired chest,
but they swear I look young for twenty-one—
just a boy is what they say

and want.

Gardenias from a Biloxi florist float in a
chipped glass bowl,
petals browned by age and
lack of honest light,
boutonnieres for those who exit early.

I grow tired of the gray goatee with
yellowed teeth and an old Masonic ring,
though he's fallen quite hard for
hard-to-get me—
we're looking at photos of
stallion-sized cocks,
his fingers fondling the fabric
beneath my waist,
those equine images insuring a
quickened pace

then I'm fleeing the
scene
full of regret

a wobbling floor
a slamming door

tasting the vomit of
ginned-up youth

sickened by the smell
of dying gardenias.

Sissy Myths

Headlines spreading dread
from sea to shining sea
(Rock Hudson has AIDS,
Who'll be Next?),
t-cells dying like cold-war
commies
scripted silence sticking
to Oval Office lips.

Narrow-gated Pharisees separating
the sick for slaughter
demanding scarlet letters and
camps with clouds of smoke,
panicky parents claiming we've
poisoned the blood supply
and lurked as snakes
among their children.

To the tops
of purple mountain majesties

sissy myths push

boulders of fear and
hate.

Needle In, Needle Out

1.

Needle in, needle out

a vial of my past from a
cotton-swabbed vein—

saliva, semen, sometimes
slapstick
contact lasting a careless
minute

single digits counting
risky tricks—

Come back in a week is the plea
of these novitiates
Sisters of Mercy who've traded their habits
for masks and gloves.

2.

I saw a fortune teller once before—

we sat in a shade-drawn house,
the feel of chenille against my
prickly back

she said I'd have a pretty wife,
three kids, a job up North

her myna bird laughed as it flew
from my startled view.

3.

I wait for the 5:10 bus, shielding my eyes
against a cold November rain

wondering if the future's any clearer
when it's seen in someone's blood.

QUESTION TIME

Do you have one?

is what I ask
is what we all ask now

that we know
how it spreads.

Water Washes Hands

1.

Blood of a friend
stains concrete

his arm broken
his skull cracked—

it wasn't an eye for an eye
or a tooth for a tooth,
but Pilate's crowd that
made him cry.

2.

Cops get queasy,
telling the victim
silence is best

he'll live with
double-locked doors
and festering wounds

like a monk who dies
obeying the Rules.

3.

Bystanders think
the freer we are
the greater the threat

but what of the threat
in the onlookers' looks?

Water washes hands,
not concrete.

Out of Love

It doesn't take a minute
to wring a chicken's neck—

make the motion fluid,
then a sudden snap.

Out of love is why we do it

or so the preachers cluck
in T.V. sermons full of
pluck—

praising ancient patriarchs for
expunging errant sons,
exchanging firm salutes and
mimicking wrists that droop,
condemning boys who chicken out
of sports or guns or girls.

Which is why my father
always changed the channel

a gentle man who
never thought

to wring a chicken's neck.

I Can Usually Tell

I can usually tell.

Take for example that man whose
eyes hold mine,
selling me coffee and a day-old doughnut,
fingers touching my hand for a
furtive moment;

or the friend whose pinky ring
points and scolds,
words floating and fluttering,
punctuating sentences with chiffon;

or my red-clay cousin in his
backwoods trailer,
chewing Skoal tobacco and
sewing sequin dresses.

But I'm not quite sure about this guy
who sings in our crossroads choir,
we both read music
though I can't read him,
not when we hiked that ten-mile trail on
a foggy Blue Ridge afternoon,
not as he turned his lanky frame to see how far
I lagged behind,
not while we shared a bottle of water
between our waiting lips.

So I'm finding it
hard
late at night
to forget about him or
his smile

imagining salty scenes
during that innocent hike

quenching my thirst
before I sleep.

Beyond City Limits

A windowless bar is our
refuge from despair,
the every-other-place we
cannot go
to find the love that dares not
speak its name—

flirting, kissing, groping,
immoral and illegal
when done on public streets.

Waiters with erections
remove their clothes for
larger tips
while drag queens mock the
Reverend Falwell and his god
of bedroom inquisitions.

The dance floor drowns in
dark brown rum,
Latin beats releasing
captive heat,
fields of sugarcane
sticky and sweet—

a final call and brightened lights
break the starlit spell

forcing us to write our
names
on matchbooks torn
in haste—

figments of forgotten
Grimm
shunning pumpkins
pulled by mice.

II
STEALING LONELINESS FROM THE NIGHT

WERE THEY NORMAL? WHAT A QUESTION TO ASK!

— E.M. FORSTER, *HOWARD'S END*

Red Shoelaces in the Bible Belt, 1986

Walking along the waterfront
afraid of holding hands,
thankful that humid air
doesn't dampen giddy hopes,
choosing phrases to
flatter and impress—

unchaperoned
our words
echo past a billboard Genesis:

Therefore shall a man cleave unto his wife
and be one flesh

leading us to my Spartan camp

a bedless barrack,
milk crates, books, dust gathered in
darkened corners

where you touch the faded skin
above my thin-boned wrist
the spot that's usually hidden by a
southpaw watch.

We're lefties
lost in the rightwing South,
drinking Winn-Dixie tonic
blue-lawed without the gin,
encouraging red-laced sneakers and
thrift-store loafers
to flirt beneath a makeshift table.

It's raining when we finally kiss,
distant thunder in our ears.

All Along

We've known all along

> my mother claims as we
> talk on the phone—
> she's afraid it's something
> they did or didn't do:

*That girl who hit your head
when you were ten—
maybe that's why
you're partial to men ...*

> Her hopes rise in ludicrous shapes
> while a seven-stitch scar skips across
> my cow-licked face.

Are you and he?

> Silence stretches between us,
> a rubber band
> ready to snap—
> I'm so scared
> we don't even say

Goodbye.

> I give my answer
> later that night
>
> spooning jigsaw tight.

Flaunting It

In a parking lot

we anger a man and woman
who see us kiss.

They're flaunting it
they groan

walking away

hand in
hand.

Sacred Objects Shouldn't Leave

An orange, an orchid, a week with you
in mango-scented air

ripe papayas, royal palms,
baby elephants on
Burmese riverbanks

soup at sunrise heating
Bangkok streets
pilgrims holding empty
bowls
Sanskrit wisdom sung by
monks

holding your hand
free from fear
Thai men winking a
silent cheer

Eastern gift shops enticing
Western tourists
souvenir Buddhas wrapped in
luminous silk
airport inspectors reciting
words of warning:

*Sacred objects shouldn't
leave*

inviting those like us
to stay in Dharma bliss.

Sibyl

High above an Italian bay
I hear the tidal rhythms
of your moonlit breathing,
the almost-death of dreamless
sleep.

And so you've left me as
you did this afternoon
when I escaped Pompeian sun for
roadside shade
an acanthus camp where
artichokes and fennel
waved purple-yellow pennants—

a coin from Nero's era
was the gift you offered
for my patient waiting.

Later, at a grotto of the
Cumaean Sibyl,
you whispered
she's an ageless bitch
with teeth
a gloomy prophetess
who spurned Apollo's love
and lost eternal youth.

In after-dinner sheet-less heat
we burned our passion with possession,
the sweaty lust of bitten lips and
tethered wrists,
while a barely noticed breeze
slowly cooled our struggle against
far-off Thanatos,
the twin of tranquil sleep whose peace
eludes me with the riddle:

Which of you will be the first
to drop that coin into the ferryman's purse?

This Frozen Place

You
dragged me to this frozen place

where shivering rooms are warmed
by chattering teeth
and winter windows wear my
frowning face—

I told you I couldn't live in this
tenured tundra
my fingers numbing as I turn the pages
of American Tariff History
long-dead footnotes forgotten like
eight-track tapes—

I told you so a year ago on that
mild Virginia evening
eating Chinese takeout with a
grain of salt
finally persuaded by your
fortune-cookie codicil:

Two
subdue
the cold.

Yet I'm longing for the Southern sun
on forever-gray days
distracted by icy rinks and
sharpened skates
torn-shirted men fighting with
oversized sticks—

you've got a crush on their goalie
(a French Canadian who speaks
your childhood tongue)

and when he looks our way
you say:

His smile is a lot like
yours.

DEDICATIONS

Plato propping a door
The Inferno smoking upstairs
Trojan Women blushing behind curtains
Frankenstein dozing under Kleenex
Sappho, Catullus, and Martial
swearing in bedroom dressers—

hundreds of dog-eared volumes
lounging around the house,
slow to thaw after four long years
of snow-shoveled winters.

You and I are also
yellow-paged,
well read and scholar-slumped,
writing weighty monographs
prefaced with possessive
pronouns:

… for his forbearance
how much his support means …
… his infinite supply of patience

expressing in silent words
the love that others proclaim out loud

knowing our lives are open books

only when
our books are opened.

Closets

Contentious clutter crowds our
make-do house
windows sealed from winter cold
and Baptist heat—

the next-door neighbors greet us
when we arrive
offering peaches with
obvious relief:

We feared you might be colored

an invitation to share their
rusted prejudice
never guessing we're a pair of
Trojan horses.

A greenhouse rises despite our
hammered thumbs
the leaning sweet gum
leans no more
milquetoast turf never cedes to
street-tough weeds—

we've laid down floors and
put up screens
issuing ultimatums that chill
our cream-and-sugar colloquies:

a Roman villa is your demand,
a modern house is my reply.

Yet we deny the plaintive cries
from wrinkled pants and rumpled shirts
telling us with straight-faced irony:

*What you really need
are several more closets.*

With or Without Props

1.

The newsreels don't do it justice—
drums, trumpets, imperial eagles,

boots blackened by Nuremberg
ink, uniforms crawling across the

Zepplinfeld like dull-headed ants,
boys and men roughhousing in

pairs of Eros and Mars—

but the city itself is hidden from view,
nothing of meandering canals, medieval

walls, churches built with Teutonic bricks,
or the joyous expressions on late-summer

faces when the purity of blood
is prescribed by law.

2.

The 11:00 p.m. news doesn't do it
justice—county councilmen are rabid

with rage, the community's been
undermined, assaulted, they cannot

sit *silently*, must *vigorously* object,
traditional families are imperiled by

this *ungodly* threat—

but the pep rally's pageantry is hidden from
view, nothing of boots or banners or

flags, just a somber vote to condemn
the menace, so we're off to bed—

fooled not at all by the lack
of props.

Sticking

This Asian island spice
held in Thai food, bathtub gin,
and pirates' painful teeth

is like the bond between us—

healing, heating, stealing loneliness from
the night

becoming our secret joke
about French toast:

Whole cloves
will never stick
to battered bread

a ruined brunch from early love
when Saturdays slept especially late

the memory making us laugh
as we lie in bed

sticking
one to the other.

Making Wine

1.

Squeezing slipskin grapes,
licking pulp from sticky fingers,
knowing that our *Manischewitz*
will never grace the shelves of Jewish delis.

It's a far-flung hobby that's become
your near-obsession,
ordering dry-iced grapes whose provenance
we pin on a corkboard map,
turning our book-lined house
into an all-night bar.

We ridicule snobbish jargon,
but it pours forth:
our wine has a *nose* and *legs*,
it *breathes* and *settles lees*,
it's often *long* and *hard*.

I design the labels with well-strained humor:
*Naughty Girl Gewurztraminer, Flapper Flask
Valpolicello, Not So Petite Syrah*—
if one becomes vinegar, I'll quickly note
For Salads Only!

2.

Now you're mixing a batch
of *Pinot Noir*,
yeasty promises filling
eager bottles—
they'll sleep like drunken
sailors,
anxious to share their
latent flavors.

We laugh and chant our daily mantra:
Make Wine Not War

removing juice-covered clothes
to sample slipskin grapes.

Joined

Cars wander like
lambs of god
panting dogs find
cooler pastures,
kudzu wraps the boughs
above our sacred rites
fifteen years since that
first entwining night.

No church or clergy
just two titanium rings
a metal found in fireworks and
vows of lasting love,
we can't say *married*
so we're *joined*
forever fastened
by that Gospel word.

Icing melts under a
blistering sun
white-sugar quicksand
engulfs two tiny grooms,
children ride a rented
horse
gaiety accepted as
common course.

A Methodist revival
begins nearby
they've seen the crowd and
two men kiss

Bind Us Together

is the only hymn
we hear them sing.

Howling Alone

Pairs make better packs

lupine
saturnine

two mixed breeds
found at the pound—

you christen them
Tarquin and *Numa*,
dogs that dog us
with our likeness.

Scanning the skies for
ancient animals,
you find Orion's
canine friends,
telling me a tale of
dog-gone fate,
the Milky Way weeping
for a missing mate.

Angry, I go inside

wondering why
you're so damn sure

that I'm the
one

who'll howl alone.

Having Drinks at the Poinsett Hotel

1.

Carolina's finest hotel leading a
Southern Living life

dimmed and shuttered,
then revived with face-lift fanfare—

overstuffed chairs, pecan paneling,
wireless internet

the façade of former glory
bragging about flamboyant guests
(Liberace was our best)

welcoming Carpetbaggers on
liberal terms

securing a lasting peace by
fixing leaks.

2.

When we're finished with our drinks
my mother takes your hand

her outworn attitudes long-since
tossed aside

forgetting she was dimmed and
shuttered

then revived.

Helicopter over Hawaii

I know you hate
heights and water

but we've been up
in the air before
and held our heads
above the waves—

bowls of beans to keep the
bills obedient
coupons clipped and
coveted
roommates paying past-due
rent.

Then that year apart,
undone by the deep blue sea—
onion-skinned letters and
tin-can conversations,
followed by our whispered
benediction: *I miss you.*

Your volcanic moods
my depressive fugues

swallowing pretty pills to calm
our daily demons

yellow blue bitter sweet.

And those stares at the
rings we wear—
remember that man who asked,
Which one's the woman?

You and I up
here

still ascending

still unafraid
of the rocks beneath us.

Mahjong ("Sparrow Game")

Click-clack
the sound of chirping sparrows—

dots, *seasons*, and *bamboo*:
what would Confucius do?

After an hour of lucky tiles
you switch to top-shelf Scotch,
though I'm content to stick with
cheap martinis—

click-clack
into the narrow night
two sparrows playing.

You win another round
without a care
gloating and getting drunk on
tempting fate
always forgetting you're not alone—

you took that rock from the top
of Kilauea
assuring me it wouldn't anger
Hawaii's goddess of fire—

yet I cautioned,
Put it back.

Click-clack Chinese bric-a-brac,
winter falls to the floor

a tile that warns *Be cautious*—

but tonight it's staying
silent
refusing to say a single word

deaf to the chirps
of one sparrow winning.

III
IN DEEPEST SLEEP

THE PAIN I FEEL NOW IS THE HAPPINESS I FELT BEFORE. THAT'S THE DEAL.

—C. S. LEWIS, *A GRIEF OBSERVED*

Three Minutes, 2010

Three minutes

for me
to give the final word

three minutes

for you
to breathe your final breath

three minutes

for them
to ask again

Are you a family member?

Kindling

White coats nodding at
blue-gowned silence

you and they
humorless
in different ways

pronounced dead
as if I can't quite grasp
vowels or consonants

habeas corpus
corpus vitae
I say a brief goodbye

no spark
no flame
no smoke

until they find
the next of kin
to strike a misanthropic match

burning body
glowing embers
a fire to light your path

That's what he wanted
I reply
before I cry.

But there is no X
where I can sign
because all they see

is *just a friend.*

A Political Act

1.

A political act writes itself:

education, work, hobbies,
candid admissions
without contrition—

He's survived by his partner of
twenty-four years.

2.

Your penciled note
rests beside my trembling pen—

Dogs: They've eaten
Me: Meditating in the Zendo

and I hear you say:

Let those words be my
eight-word obit

comforting those who fear
that I'll be bloodied
if I include our dangerous truth.

3.

To be or not to be
a sentence or two
of grieving ink—

I wobble like the table
for a wayward moment,
shifting my weight
on shaky legs:

a political act rights itself.

Postmortems

Condolences arrive
in casket-hued italics,
dry-eyed platitudes
as stoic as
American Gothic,
men and women
in Hallmark pairs,
the natural order
remaining
farmhouse still.

These cosmetic cards
are bought at corner
drugstores,
where
ointments,
salves,
and purges
claim they'll
cure
my deepest urges.

This More of Me

We taught well hidden
in plain unhidden sight,
stealing glances across an
academic lawn,
avoiding students whose
favorite quotes
were brimstone anecdotes.

Now you're gone
but I'm still here,
sunk in stained-glass
sorrow,
my life laid bare
by church-filled prayers.

Coteries of votaries
praise your
classroom quirks—
a bearded kid
in faded jeans
applauds your
awesome grasp
of Latin grammar
(it was *infinitum*).

Yet mine is the perfect loss
they can't accept,
convinced by pounding pulpits
that our love
was nothing more
than salty pillars.

Knowing this more of me,
perhaps they'll bury
both of us

crosses
like our nooses
dangling from their unbent necks.

Without Permission

I'll take the things you left
without permission

from your room forever
stilled:

old exams and bottles
of diazepam

rucksacks, hardtack,
shotgun shells

beefcake pin-ups and
unshucked nuts

ticket stubs, hockey skates,
an ankle brace

Astrology for Queers
and lists of solar years—

I'll move them to a corner
of my cobwebbed thoughts

where they'll live in poems
death possessed

reminding me
you left without permission.

Clocks

You bought so many of
them

tick-tocking
chiming
alarming

they shine as if time
were just another toy

wound up
wind down.

I cannot find their directions
or any guide for life without you

which is why your clocks
are prone to disagree:

I eat in Boston
read in Paris
sleep in Chicago.

If your ghost
ever wants to meet me

we'll surely be unsynchronized

running fast
running late

missing
our mis-timed date.

Left in the Pack

Lies on your desk an open pack
lies when it says you haven't died
dust to dust
ashtray full
you've disappeared—
exhaled
like a puff of Marlboro Lights.

I was the Surgeon General
you were General Grant
cigar in mouth
bearded Union president
old memories
pneumonia
throw that pack away.

You said *smokes*
I said *cigarettes*
fags never crossed our lips.

I'll Wait

I'll wait
to wash these clothes

the ones we shared
with threadbare pride

cotton shirts
wool sweaters
unembarrassed polyester

smelling of
onion rings,
Buffalo wings,
and all those
mornings
when we recalled

our perfect fit
the night before.

Along a Backyard Path

1.

Along a backyard path
beset by metaphors—

snowbird heliotropes
ignoring Mason and Dixon

smuggled New York seeds
rising into catalpas

fence-destroying grapes
cursing homemade wine

courageous pansies
parading campy colors

Venus flytraps
waiting with widened mouths

pathetic pawpaws
neglecting newborn fruit

fan-tailed palms
bowing to Easter lilies.

2.

When my circuit
comes full circle,
I mourn your death anew

the one who nurtured
plants and me

unmetaphorically.

Adrift

1.

I remember
the naked touch of night:

restless legs and
grinding teeth,
feet floundering in
twisted sheets,
calloused fingers
tracing the cove
beneath your
Adam's apple.

2.

In the chlorinated sea
of backyard pools
I learned to save
a life or two:

an encircling arm
calms the panic
and keeps the lungs
ballooned with air.

It's no different
in the ocean

of a bed.

Dreams, You Said

I greet you in soliloquies
but you rarely speak—

no questions about me
the dogs
the leaking roof
or the plants
I've nearly killed.

Last night
the two of us
lay silent and still
like that Etruscan sarcophagus
we saw so long ago—

a smiling couple
sculpted on top
pointing to the great beyond.

Will you return again?

Dreams
you said
would be our only afterlife.

Backseat Ashes

I drive the truck you loved
then left—

twelve years old and marred by
scratched green paint
home for your dashboard Buddha
and that triumphant sticker:

I'm a Son of Union Veterans!

You also left yourself in a
backseat box,
cremated corpse
like chalkboard dust,
giving me the chance to share
your blackened humor
over blackened fish,
telling all who wonder
what you might think
about those Rebel rants
bereft of Yankee sense:

Go ask him—
he's in his truck.

Boxes

They were the loyal playmates
of my sunburnt summers

This End Up
Handle with Care
Contents May Shift

a boy marked
fragile
hiding in cardboard
castles.

Staples and tape
mend holes and tears,
but I no longer fit
inside those corrugated shells—

arms stick out
legs get tangled
feet fall asleep.

Failing to find a box
for my unnamed self,
I damn the command
to *Please check one:*

[ ] single
[ ] married
[ ] divorced
[ ] widowed

Sands of Kitty Hawk

1.

We imagined a Grecian war along
this tar-heeled shore
reenacting midday moments
from Homer's Song of Ilium:

Achilles and Patroclus
forever young
removing armor with
heated haste
parching tongues suddenly
ablaze
lovers posing for a
painted vase.

Evening pelicans woke us from our
sweat-entangled sleep
and as we climbed to higher ground
two women
weathered and lined
wandered across our salt-spray path
speaking in silent tongues and
knowing eyes
their dovetailed devotion inspiring
the vow we took
to walk this beach again

you and I gray with age.

2.

But death has severed the you from us
shedding blood and myths of innocence

leaving me alone
to mourn the sands of Kitty Hawk

a widow's walk amid the crashing waves.

Thinking Barefoot Thoughts

Food I've ignored
for weeks or more
spoils in cold
nostalgic air,
pungent secrets
sealed behind
an old refrigerator door.

Mayonnaise, pickles, and
ketchup last the longest,
reminding me of casseroles
consumed at midnight
when two of us
not one
conducted barefoot raids
on foil-covered containers—

when milk and bread
were never left for dead.

The Castle

We knew that it'd be tough—

tough for us to
bear
a town as grim as
this—
this righteous
garden
on guard against the
hiss.

There was only one—

one unguarded
bar
a club where we could
go—
go but never
went
before that place
was spent.

The Castle was the name it took—

took from Kafka's
title
seems quite
unlikely—
unlikely as any
space
for finding local
grace.

A Latin meaning is far more apt—

apt to make it
clear
the reason we'd never
scoffed—
scoffed at *castle's*
root
which means to be
cut off.

IV
Reviving Rhythms

I'VE ALWAYS BEEN MYSELF ... ONLY NOW I *SEEM* MYSELF. THAT'S THE IMPORTANT THING. I HAVE LEARNED HOW TO SEEM.

—ALAN BENNETT, *THE MADNESS OF GEORGE III*

Click to Enter

1.

I *Click to Enter*

hands shaking and
knees jiggling
scrolling through full-frontal
photos
painful blues provoked by
strip-tease gigolos—

Date a Guy Half Your Age appears in
covered-dish script
accompanied by *Dirt-Cheap Rates for
Uncut Twinks*
high-priced hustlers with
porn-like prowess,
causing me to switch
to a site in gray-haired type,
where I search *Must Likes*
for Thai food, movies, cuddling—

but fail to find a single
Match
stuck instead with several pics
of Slick-Stud's penis,
his tattooed phallus asking
Wanna Fuck?
an old Germanic verb as stone-fence hard
as this unlikely suitor.

2.

Two canines curl
in fitful sleep,
impatient with these
prancing satyrs
who take my time
to beg and whine—

so I *Log Out*

content with dogs on
leashes

nothing online.

Dancing in L.A.

Dancing in L.A.
is a poem becoming
self-aware,
scanning lines for
reviving rhythms,
finding followers of
Narcissus:

Olympian gods
with marble chests,
flashing Delphic teeth that
blind like sonnets
soaked in bleach

youthful mouths
demanding rigid diction,
wisdom flowing
from sacred springs
as they discuss
their nipple rings

barside bonbons
arrayed in jaded
threesomes,
filled with contempt
for *blushing pilgrims*—

telling me
I'm old fashioned

even Elizabethan

because I prefer
the art of courting

fully clothed.

Self Fashioning

Auditioning myself for
later tonight:

a pink pullover finds the
feminine within

a revealing tee outlines muscles
for hungry looks

a rugby shirt conceals the
lack of abs underneath

a designer tie seduces
younger smiles

a *Gourmet* apron hides
Betty-Crocker hips

a pool-cued plaid makes me
oh-so-lesbian.

The mirror laughs and sighs
at my discarded clothes

confessing fondness
for a former self

the one that fits me
like a glove

without the need for
matching hat.

Basic Math

I'm milling among the sherry-
stemmed women,
glancing at men with cock-
tails stirred and shaken.

They say we're five percent
so I decide to calculate:

dreadlocks and no locks,
philanthropists and philanderers,
the dry witted outwitting the dry cleaned,
mirthless ministers and drunken matadors—

forty men including me.

I'll look
for the only other one

to share a laugh
a kiss
a life

using fingers and our toes

to do the math
of every touch.

Dated

I'm considered a fossil at fifty-one
except by men who like buffets and
think my name is *Doc*.

This one's from a little lardy spot
on the *Palmetto State* map—

dramatic gestures straight from
silent films
Valentino's ego without
the eyes or shoulders
endless monologues about venison,
moonshine, how his second wife
pissed him off—

and, if you didn't guess, he's an
expert on politics and guns,
opinions uninformed by a
single book—
just grunting and painting
on damp cave walls.

It's much too late
for a quick escape,
so I nod politely
at his ceaseless droning

adding him to the list of men
whose love for themselves
has the gumless taste

of day old grits.

The Flower of Southern Manhood

While I'm stopped at a long red light
a man runs naked around his truck

hooting hollering dangling

boisterous bravado that's the picture
of Pickett's charge:

red hair
white flesh
hill-country caterwauling

letting every little thing
hang out,
yet lacking the bravery of
those who died,
men with clothes blown off
by the fiery breath
of a Union cannonade.

So when he sees me look
unblinking
at the flower of his southern
manhood

he retreats

bluster gone
bayonet sheathed

leaving the battlefield
to me

the one he mistakes

for his mortal
enemy.

I Can Leave Anything

A haughty
youth
commands the
register,
withholding
his smile
as I approach,
dismissing me
with Adonic
disdain.

Next to racks
of gum and mints
plastic wrappers
hide glossy
covers,
ample cleavage
concealed
from customers
and cashiers.

I am likewise—

wise to the
looks
that never pierce
my aging skin,
teflon armor
repelling
erotic ardor.

In reply
to the
deceitful receipt
*(Have a
nice day!)*,
I place my
pride
on a royal
litter
so I can
leave

anything but bitter.

Hunting (Muscle Beach, CA)

These flexing exhibitions
are a carnivore's delight,
but even vegans
stop to gawk—
biceps, triceps, quadriceps
baby oiled and darkly tanned,
muscles that fuel a fetish
when testosterone runs amok.

Men from Little Rock
who visit human zoos
use camouflage and
cans of beer
to hide their
boyhood fears—

they'll brag back home in
Arkansas
about how close they got
to untamed creatures

how they saw
a blond one
with leonine hair
on broadened shoulders

whose gaze I catch
and hold

lion-like

the hunter
and the hunted—

I'm never quite sure
which is which.

One Nightstand

One nightstand
sitting beside my messy bed—

it wobbles beneath the lamp
whose base is a grinning ape,
unaware of motley misfits
that crowd its unhinged drawer:

Canadian coins
plastic chopsticks
baby aspirin

and names of men
who charge to entertain.

If I summoned one of them
he'd likely be a simian
(feeling kinship with the lamp)
or a lithesome winsome youth
who'd move his lips
before he spoke.

Then there'd be
that awkward chat
about the angles of attack,
and whether we'd do it
in the dark
or give the neighbors
quite a start—
not to mention the
disaffected dogs
who'd bark in backyard exile.

And after our *pas de deux*
of primal grunts
I'd search for words unsaid
to animate that one-night stand
sitting beside my messy bed.

Pounding on Top

Arriving at dawn
beating the heat
boots above
stripped to the waist by noon
four men peeling a frying-pan roof
shingles falling beside my house
pounding on top
I'm shaking below
hammers shouting call-and-response
threatening storms
quickening tempo
muscles stiffening
a cooling shower
skin and hair the color of wheat
wary eyes finally meet.

A Woman with Becoming Features

Born again
from *him* to *her*,
tricky transitions
she's handled with grace,
feats we honor
by eating a feast—

bbq ribs staining our lips,
collards succumbing to grease,
banana cream pie lying in wait.

Our busboy quakes like the
Holy Ghost,
he hasn't a clue what to do
with my feminine friend—
she's very pert
in a form-fitting skirt,
batting a lash
to land a catch—
perhaps it's her wig
that makes people pause,
her stylish strands
refusing to budge.

She's a man becoming a woman,
a woman with becoming features—

her Episcopal priest says
*God doesn't mind
unless you're gay*

but she pays no nevermind
to church-going folk

they're blind to a dragonfly

spreading her
wings.

Choosing Fruit

Acquaintances in cozy pairs
point at barrels and crates,
claiming I lack the knack
for choosing fruit—

Forgive a bruise or two
Wash them more than once
Peel the skin if you prefer
Swallow the seeds without concern
Just look hard enough to suit your tastes.

So let me humor them:

peaches put on weight
kiwis seldom shave
lemons always criticize
figs feel inadequate
melons are messy
berries demand a brunch
grapes get drunk
apples wave flags
and bananas—

do I really need to say?

Hard enough
is never enough.

By Mixing Pink and Blue

Quiet evenings
whisper in my ear,
urging me to paint
the brown-tipped petals
from my gin-spilled youth.

I liberate these memories
with squinting brushstrokes,
using water and a rag
to erase my past mistakes.

A lavender rose brightens the
gloom of night
it's from a little boy who smiles that
gap-toothed smile I had at five:

he plays with beat-up trucks
and wears a strand of costume pearls,
fingernails encrusted with
playground dirt
(or powered sugar when
he bakes).

I hear the noisy hail of an
unexpected storm
the tempest of black and white
disturbing a rainbow life.

Yet the rose retains
its brilliant hue

the one I paint

by mixing
pink and blue.

Unnatural

It wasn't as if
belief had died
despite the fact
I'd put away
my childish thoughts:

I never forget
the lionized den
of Daniel's faith
or David's love
for close-knit Jonathan.

But I wouldn't accept
the made-up words
that King James used
to strike me dead.

And so they've barred
the door—
calling me *unnatural*,
rotten to the very core.

I've studied floor plans,
peered through windows,
tried all the locks—
they guard the building
like a hawk.

And when I mention
an apostle's claim
that long-haired men
possess *unnatural* curls,
they're quick to admit
from behind that bolted door
how glad they are
to disregard

those bits of foolish lore.

Once Before

Hawksbill Creek counts cold December nights,
rushing along winter-berry banks until it reaches Christmas Eve,
listening to hard-shell Baptists sing their self-assuring hymns,
antebellum voices rising above this vanquished valley,
a Confederate cache of tin-type tales,
overwrought epics worshipping the over-praised past,
accompanied by the scene that hangs in my cheap motel,
a pitiful painting honoring the barefoot boys
who died to save the milk-white caste of their Scotch-Irish skin,
the desk clerk resurrecting the long-lost Cause,
reserving her righteous cant for Mexicans, welfare, and all them gays,
telling an empty lobby *We've been invaded once before*—
and as I leave the town on New Year's Day,
driving past signs with floating sombreros,
I give one last wink to my favorite pigeon-stained statue:
a Civil War general who died a bachelor.

Down South, 2015

I stir
from intravenous sleep

the surgeon prodding me
(swollen and immodest)
with ice-cold hands of
mild amusement:

*Nothing was where
it ought to be.*

Antiseptic solitude
inscribes a lonely arc
of four long years—

no kiss, no touch,
no love
just re-stuffing that hole down
south
the one they fixed when I was
ten days old
a teeny preemie with a
hateful hernia
feeling the pain that cuts through
skin and heart.

So fuck
this dropped-pants awkwardness—

I'm getting dressed and
hobbling home

far from lost
far from fear

living at peace
with life Down South.

Acknowledgments

In *Madame Bovary*, the character Rodolphe Boulanger observes: "The human language is like a cracked kettle on which we beat out a tune for a dancing bear, when we hope with our music to move the stars." In my efforts to move stars instead of bears, many people have been indispensible.

Patricia Horan was patient, yet demanding as my initial mentor. She helped me to replace a cracked kettle with a better instrument. At the other end of what turned out to be a four-year process, Paulette Alden, Gil Allen, Brian Lupo, Ted Puntanen, and Bill Rogers offered invaluable comments and suggestions on the entire manuscript. The same is true for Judy Bainbridge, who supplied the additional benefits of delicious meals on a regular basis.

Numerous people supplied encouragement and other assistance. They include Stella Barnello, Scott Becker, Jon Chastain, Denise Crockett, Jim Currier, Mary Fairbairn, Sallie Fallaw, Tom Fallaw, Judy Grisel, Erin Hahn, Nelly Hecker, Ciara Henderson, Eileen Henderson, Wayne Hoffman, Alan Lessoff, Jane Love, Reece Lyerly, Ross McClain, Jane Mannion Henderson, Elaine Nocks, Amy Oney, Jay Oney, Si Pearman, Ed Prior, Stel Prior, Lesley Quast, Freeman Rogers, Carrie Seigler, Mark Sullivan, Carol Sutton, Brendan Tapley, Branden Tensley, Paul Thomas, and Susan Thomas.

Some of my poetry has previously appeared in *Chelsea Station Magazine* and *Smartish Pace*. The high standards and gracious solicitude of these two journals provided me with timely votes of confidence. In regard to spiritual gratitude, I owe many thanks to the Greenville Quaker Meeting. Having spent much of my youth attending churches that excoriated the "homosexual lifestyle," I am happy to have found peace and acceptance among Friends.

This book would not have been possible without the hard work and sage advice of Jill Hendrix and Vally Sharpe at FPS. They have guided this project from manuscript to publication. Words cannot do them justice.

Judith Alexander was the first person to suggest that I try my hand at writing poetry. From the outset, she provided a sympathetic and sensitive ear. Her enthusiasm was unflagging. I could not have asked for a better muse—or friend.

My earliest memories involve my brother. We have shared a special bond since childhood (partly because we are fraternal twins), a bond that continues to highlight our similarities, while also celebrating our differences. He is not just my brother; he is also my friend and advocate.

I spent twenty-four years with a loving partner. His life and death have shaped many of my poems. If, as a result of those poems, readers gain a better understanding of him, then they will also have a better understanding of *me*.

About the Poet

A. SCOTT HENDERSON is the William R. Kenan Jr. Professor of Education at Furman University. Born and raised in West Palm Beach, Florida, he is the author/editor of four non-fiction books. His poems have previously appeared in *Chelsea Station Magazine* and *Smartish Pace*.

When he's not writing poetry, Scott enjoys hiking, painting, singing, playing the trumpet, and black & white photography. He has lived in Greenville, South Carolina since 1995.

To order additional copies of

Gin and Gardenias

please contact the publisher at
www.FPSPublishing.com

Gin and Gardenias
is also available as an ebook
via Amazon, Nook and Kobo.

www.ingramcontent.com/pod-product-compliance
Lightning Source LLC
Chambersburg PA
CBHW040416100526
44588CB00022B/2848